Original title:
Love's Revival

Copyright © 2024 Swan Charm
All rights reserved.

Author: Sebastian Sarapuu
ISBN HARDBACK: 978-9916-89-871-0
ISBN PAPERBACK: 978-9916-89-872-7
ISBN EBOOK: 978-9916-89-873-4

Awakening the Heart's Whisper

In silence, the heart beats true,
A gentle call, a light breaks through.
Whispers of love, soft and clear,
Awakening hope, dispelling fear.

With faith's embrace, we find our light,
Guided by spirits, pure and bright.
Each moment graced, a chance to grow,
In the warmth of love, our souls in flow.

Sacred Embrace of Renewal

In the stillness, life finds its way,
A sacred touch, a brand new day.
With every dawn, we breathe in deep,
A promise kept, a joy to reap.

Cleansed by tears, the spirit sings,
Renewal blooms; hope takes wing.
In nature's arms, we find our rest,
In the sacred path, we are blessed.

The Divine Tapestry of Affection

Threads of love weave through the night,
A tapestry, both soft and bright.
Each heart a patch, unique in hue,
Stitched together, old and new.

In tender moments, grace flows free,
A bond unbroken, you and me.
With every thread, our stories blend,
In divine love, we find our mend.

Celestial Reunion of Souls

Stars aligned in a cosmic dance,
Souls entwined in a sacred chance.
In the quiet, our spirits soar,
Reunited, forevermore.

With open hearts, we share the light,
Guiding each other through the night.
In celestial realms, we are whole,
A joyous union, one sacred soul.

Whispers of the Miraculous Reunion

In shadows soft, where silence dwells,
Two hearts converge, as heaven swells.
A sacred call, a gentle breeze,
In love's embrace, our spirits ease.

Through trials past, we've walked apart,
Yet faith has woven us, heart to heart.
The light descends, a golden thread,
In grateful whispers, our souls are fed.

Each tear we've shed, a lesson learned,
In patience, hope, the fire burned.
With every prayer, a beacon bright,
Guiding us home, through darkest night.

Rejoice, O spirits, in this grace,
In joyous laughter, find your place.
For love unites, as rivers flow,
In sacred bonds, our faith will grow.

With open arms, we now embrace,
The miracle of time and space.
Through whispered vows, our trust renews,
In gentle light, our path we choose.

A Divine Accord of Hearts Transformed

In morning mist, the dawn arrives,
With tender light, our spirit thrives.
A gentle touch, a sacred song,
In harmony, we both belong.

From ashes rise, in faith we're found,
In grace adorned, our souls unbound.
Transformed by love, we stand anew,
With every breath, we pledge our view.

In silence shared, our hearts entwine,
Each promise keeps, a bond divine.
Through trials faced, our spirits soar,
In love's embrace, we want for more.

With whispered prayers and hopeful grace,
We seek to find our sacred place.
In every glance, in every smile,
The divine accord will last awhile.

Together now, our spirits rise,
In unity, we touch the skies.
For every moment, every sigh,
Transforms our hearts to reach on high.

The Blessed Reunion of Kindred Spirits

Upon the hill, where shadows fade,
Two souls rejoice, in light arrayed.
In timeless embrace, they come alive,
With whispers soft, the spirits thrive.

Through trials faced, they found their way,
In love embraced, they chose to stay.
With open hearts and eyes aglow,
The blessings flow, as rivers go.

In every laugh, in every tear,
They share the weight, they share the cheer.
With grace surrounded, they stand tall,
In unity, they will not fall.

With sacred vows, their spirits sing,
A celebration of everything.
A constellation, a radiant light,
Guiding souls home, through day and night.

Now hand in hand, they walk the way,
In holy joy, they choose to stay.
For every heartbeat echoes clear,
In blessed reunion, love is near.

Reflections of Faith in Tides of Togetherness

In still waters, prayers rise,
Hearts united, none disguise.
Each wave whispers trust divine,
Together, our spirits shine.

Through storms, we find our grace,
In faith's light, we embrace.
Guided by love's gentle hand,
Together, we take our stand.

With every tide, hope renews,
In quiet moments, love ensues.
A bond forged in sacred light,
In darkness, we are the bright.

With open hearts, we soar high,
On wings of faith, we never die.
Together, we journey, all as one,
In unity, we have won.

In tranquil shores, we abide,
In each other, we confide.
Tides of love, forever flow,
In this togetherness, we grow.

Eternal Thread of Devoted Spirits

In the loom of life, we weave,
Threads of faith, we all believe.
Bound by love, each soul aligned,
In this fabric, peace we find.

Through trials faced, we intertwine,
In every tear, your hand in mine.
A sacred bond that time won't break,
Eternal thread, for hope's sake.

Whispers linger in the night,
Guiding stars, our hearts take flight.
Spirit strong, we carry on,
In devotion, we are drawn.

With every breath, a promise made,
In your light, my fears will fade.
Together in this sacred dance,
Devoted spirits, life's romance.

In harmony, we rise and fall,
United voices, love's sweet call.
Eternal thread, forever spun,
In divine embrace, we are one.

Reclaiming the Sacred Garden

In the garden where we dream,
Seeds of faith begin to gleam.
With each prayer, a flower grows,
In love's embrace, the spirit flows.

Tend the soil with gentle hands,
Reclaiming hope in sacred lands.
Pulling weeds of doubt away,
In trust, we find the light of day.

With water drawn from solace deep,
In every heart, we plant and keep.
Together, we watch love bloom,
In this garden, dispel the gloom.

Underneath the golden sun,
All are welcome, everyone.
United in our sacred toil,
In harmony, we bless the soil.

Through seasons change, we walk in faith,
Nurturing dreams, we've all laid wraith.
In this garden, we shall thrive,
Together, we feel so alive.

The Alchemy of Forging New Beginnings

In the heart of night, we stand,
Crafting dreams with steady hand.
From the ashes, rise anew,
In our souls, the flame shines through.

Every end a fertile ground,
In silence, hear the sacred sound.
What was lost now finds its way,
In morning's light, there dawns a day.

With each choice, new paths unfold,
In the warmth of love, we mold.
Forging bonds that time won't sever,
In this truth, we find forever.

In the crucible of the heart,
Each moment plays a vital part.
Transformation in the fire,
From the depths, we all aspire.

With open hearts, we forge ahead,
In unity, by love we're led.
Together, we ignite the spark,
Creating light within the dark.

The Testament of Revived Vulnerability

In shadows deep, we bare our heart,
A testament of hope, a brand new start.
With every tear, a seed is sown,
In vulnerability, we find our own.

In tender trust, we share our pain,
A sacred bond, like falling rain.
With open arms, we greet the night,
Our wounds shall weave the fabric bright.

In whispered prayers, our spirits rise,
A chorus sweet beneath the skies.
With honesty, our souls entwine,
In each embrace, the light will shine.

Through trials faced, we learn to see,
The strength that lies in honesty.
In brokenness, the truth is found,
A circle forged on common ground.

Resilience grows where we declare,
In fragile moments, love laid bare.
The testament we carry forth,
Is of a life reborn in worth.

Elysian Roads to Connection

Along the paths where spirits roam,
We seek the place we can call home.
In sacred space, our hearts align,
Elysian roads that intertwine.

With every step, divinity calls,
In gentle whispers, love enthralls.
A tapestry of souls embraced,
In strains of hope, compassion graced.

The laughter shared, the tears we shed,
Create a bond that cannot dread.
As shadows fade, and light breaks through,
Elysian roads bring joy anew.

Through trials faced, we find our way,
In connection forged, we softly sway.
Together woven, hand in hand,
We walk the path, united stand.

In sacred circles, hearts ignite,
Illuminating the darkest night.
With every breath, we weave the thread,
Of love that leads where angels tread.

Wings of Celestial Affinity

In realms above, our spirits soar,
With wings of light, we seek for more.
Celestial dance, a journey vast,
In unity, our shadows cast.

Through endless skies, with grace we glide,
In harmony, our hearts collide.
Each whispered prayer, a gentle breeze,
Wings of affinity bring us ease.

In sacred moments, time stands still,
As love transcends the human will.
With every beat, our spirits sing,
The joy of flight, the peace we bring.

Through trials faced, we rise anew,
In sisterhood, where skies are blue.
With every dawn, our hopes take flight,
Wings of celestial, pure delight.

Together woven in cosmic blend,
The light of love shall never end.
In every heart, a spark shall gleam,
Wings of affinity, a shared dream.

The Chapel of Reconciled Souls

In sacred halls where echoes dwell,
The chapel stands, a peace-filled shell.
With open hearts, we gather near,
In whispered thoughts, our prayers sincere.

Through trials shared, our spirits mend,
In love's embrace, we find our friend.
With every tear, a flow of grace,
The chapel shines, a sacred space.

In harmony, our voices rise,
A symphony that fills the skies.
With every note, a bond reclaims,
The chapel bears our hopeful names.

In moments hushed, the truth revealed,
Our wounds, together, gently healed.
With every step, we walk as one,
In reconciliation, life's begun.

Through every storm, we lift our gaze,
In silent prayer, our hearts ablaze.
The chapel of our reconciled souls,
A timeless grace that forever holds.

Seraphic Flames Rekindled

In the quiet night, angels sing,
Their voices soar, pure offerings.
Heaven's fire ignites the soul,
Reviving dreams, making us whole.

With every whisper, love flows bright,
Touching hearts, illuminating night.
In warmth embraced, we rise anew,
Seraphic flames dance, ever true.

In shadows cast, hope shall gleam,
Faith ignites each tender dream.
With open arms, we find our place,
Within the glow of boundless grace.

Let spirits soar on wings of light,
Guided by stars that shine so bright.
Each moment cherished, a sacred sign,
In unity, our souls entwine.

With every prayer, the heavens sigh,
Awakening love that cannot die.
Through trials faced, we stand as one,
In seraphic flames, our journey's begun.

Anointed by the Touch of Grace

From hands divine, blessings flow,
Anointed hearts, in love we grow.
Each tender touch, a sacred gift,
Lifetimes changed, our spirits lift.

In valleys low, we find the key,
Unlocking hope, setting us free.
With every step, let kindness lead,
Finding joy in each small deed.

The gentle rain, a heavenly sign,
Nurtures souls with love divine.
In whispered prayers, we seek the light,
Guided forth by faith's pure sight.

Beneath the stars, we gather near,
Sharing whispers, casting fear.
With hearts entwined, we claim our place,
Anointed by the touch of grace.

As dawn breaks forth, new life ignites,
A symphony of hope takes flight.
In every moment, love's embrace,
We walk together, filled with grace.

Embracing the Light After the Storm

After shadows fall, light appears,
Washing away our doubts and fears.
In the stillness, solace found,
Hearts reborn on sacred ground.

Through tempests fierce, we learn to soar,
Resilient souls, forevermore.
With faith as our unwavering guide,
We embrace the light, with arms spread wide.

Each drop of rain, a lesson learned,
In every struggle, our spirits burned.
Yet from the ashes, we rise anew,
Embracing hope, in skies so blue.

The dawn awakens, a gentle grace,
Kissing the wounds, each weary face.
With open hearts, we find our way,
Together, we greet the brand new day.

In unity, we shall remain,
Building strength through joy and pain.
Embracing light, together we stand,
After the storm, hand in hand.

Harmonic Ascendancy of Passion

In the temple of the heart, flames rise,
Passion's spark ignites the skies.
With every note, the spirit sings,
A harmonic joy that love brings.

With ardor bright, our voices blend,
In sacred rhythms, we ascend.
Each heartbeat echoes, timeless and true,
Harmonic tales of me and you.

Through trials faced, our souls unite,
Guided by love's eternal light.
In every challenge, a wonder found,
We rise together, breaking ground.

With fervent dreams, we reach for more,
Opening wide the celestial door.
In this ascent, our spirits soar,
Harmonic passion, forevermore.

As melodies weave through the air,
We find our hope, laid bare.
In symphonies of love's embrace,
We dance together, finding grace.

Faith's Tender Allure

In shadows deep, we seek the light,
A gentle whisper through the night.
With every breath, our spirits sing,
In faith's embrace, we find our wings.

The dawn unfolds, a golden hue,
Each promise made, pure and true.
In trials faced, we stand as one,
With hearts ablaze, we greet the sun.

The sacred path is paved in grace,
In every tear, we find His face.
With every step, we hold Him near,
In faith's sweet lull, we cast our fear.

Through valleys low and mountains high,
Our spirits rise, we touch the sky.
In love divine, we find our rest,
In faith's soft arms, we are truly blessed.

Together strong, we walk the way,
In prayerful whispers, night and day.
With open hearts, we share the call,
In faith's tender allure, we shall not fall.

Celestial Dance of Two Souls

In starlit nights, our spirits soar,
Beyond the world, we seek for more.
With every heartbeat, love's refrain,
In celestial dance, we break each chain.

Two souls entwined, a sacred bond,
In whispered dreams, we grow beyond.
With eyes aglow, we blaze the trail,
In cosmic grace, our hearts prevail.

The universe sings a timeless tune,
In every phase, like sun and moon.
With every step, we glide in trust,
In love's embrace, it's pure and just.

We weave a tapestry of light,
In shadows cast, we share our might.
With every moment, love's decree,
In this divine dance, we are set free.

Hand in hand, through storms and calm,
In sacred spaces, we find our balm.
Together bound, as stories unfold,
In the celestial dance, we are consoled.

Grace Unfurled in Silent Prayers

In quiet moments, whispers rise,
A sacred bond that never dies.
With every heartbeat, hopes ascends,
In grace unfurled, our spirit mends.

The gentle hush invites the soul,
In silent prayers, we are made whole.
With lifted hearts, we seek the truth,
In every breath, there's holy proof.

With eyes closed tight, we journey deep,
In sacred stillness, love we keep.
The world may rage, but here we stand,
In grace unveiled, we hold His hand.

In every trial, we find the way,
In muted strength, we rise and pray.
With faith as guide, our spirits soar,
In grace's glow, we long for more.

Together bound by threads of light,
In silent prayers, we claim our right.
Each whispered wish, a step we take,
In grace unfurled, our souls awake.

The Miraculous Touch of Affection

In tender moments, hearts collide,
With gentle hands, love's grace abides.
Through trials faced, we find our fate,
In miraculous touch, we celebrate.

The world may falter, storms may rage,
In love's embrace, we turn the page.
With every gaze, a spark divine,
In affection's glow, we intertwine.

Each laugh we share, a precious gift,
In softness found, our spirits lift.
With open hearts, we brave the tide,
In miraculous touch, we do not hide.

Through time's embrace, we learn to see,
In love's reflection, we are set free.
With every tear, a blessing flows,
In tender touch, affection grows.

Together bound in this embrace,
In love's sweet dance, we find our place.
With every heartbeat, we ignite,
In miraculous touch, we find the light.

Cherished Echoes from Sacred Spaces

In quiet chambers where light resides,
Whispers of hope in faith abide.
Each prayer spoken, a soft caress,
Filling hearts with gentle rest.

Within the silence, spirits soar,
Connecting souls forevermore.
In every echo, love is found,
A sacred bond forever bound.

The light of dawn warms weary souls,
Guiding us towards higher goals.
With trust and courage, we unite,
In cherished echoes, we find our light.

Beneath the stars, we lift our gaze,
Singing softly in endless praise.
In moments shared, our faith ignites,
A tapestry of hope in heights.

Through trials faced, we stand as one,
In sacred spaces, love's begun.
Together weaving joy divine,
In cherished echoes, hearts align.

Woven in Threads of Grace

In the fabric of life, we find our place,
Hearts entwined, woven in threads of grace.
Each moment treasured, a stitch in time,
Unified voices in harmony's rhyme.

Through trials and joys, our spirits blend,
Every heartbeat, a message to send.
In the warmth of faith, we find our way,
Woven together, come what may.

In the quiet whispers, love is sown,
A tapestry rich, from seeds we've grown.
In sacred gatherings, our souls embrace,
Woven in unity, bathed in grace.

With hands uplifted, we seek the light,
Guided by purpose, shining bright.
In every prayer, a promise flows,
Woven in grace, our spirit grows.

Together we journey, side by side,
In the dance of faith, we will abide.
Our stories told through love's embrace,
Bound eternally, woven in grace.

The Grace of Souls Entwined

In the garden of life, we flourish and bloom,
Souls entwined, dispelling all gloom.
In love's embrace, we find our light,
A beacon shining through the night.

With every heartbeat, our spirits rise,
A chorus lifted to the skies.
In unity's warmth, we find our way,
The grace of souls entwined, we pray.

Through storms we venture, hand in hand,
Faithful companions in a promised land.
In shared reflections, our truth is shown,
In the grace of souls, we are not alone.

With kindness spoken, we heal the rift,
Celebrating life, the greatest gift.
In every moment, love's embrace,
The grace of souls, a timeless grace.

Together we rise, like dawn's ascent,
In sacred unity, our lives are spent.
In every heartbeat, a sacred sign,
Forever bound, the grace of souls entwined.

Manifesting Blessings of Togetherness

In the circle of life, we gather near,
Manifesting blessings, casting out fear.
Each joyful laugh, a song we share,
In moments sacred, we show we care.

The light of kindness fuels our flight,
Bringing forth love, igniting the night.
In unity's strength, we find our ground,
Manifesting blessings in love profound.

Through trials faced, we lift each other,
In every heart, spirit's mother.
Hand in hand, we chase the dawn,
In togetherness, fears are gone.

In shared embraces, we find our peace,
With every struggle, love's release.
Together we stand, a shining crew,
Manifesting blessings, bright and true.

With grateful hearts, we gather as one,
In harmony forged, life's journey begun.
In every moment, our spirits sing,
Manifesting togetherness, joy we bring.

Chosen Blessings of the Heart

In the silence of dawn, grace whispers low,
Hearts entwined, in faith we grow.
Every blessing, a light divine,
Guides us forth, on paths we find.

In shadows cast, His love will beam,
Filling souls with hope's sweet dream.
Through trials faced, our spirits rise,
Chosen, we bask in heavenly ties.

Through each tear and every smile,
We walk this sacred, holy mile.
In unity, His mercy flows,
A garden of grace that ever grows.

With every heartbeat, songs unfold,
Stories of faith, in whispers told.
In the tapestry of life we weave,
Chosen blessings, we believe.

A symphony of joy and grace,
In each embrace, we find our place.
Together bound by love's sweet art,
In every moment, the chosen heart.

Psalms of Rediscovery

In stillness found, we seek the light,
A journey inward, day and night.
With open hearts and eyes anew,
We sing the psalms, our voices true.

Through valleys deep and mountains high,
The echoes call, a sacred sigh.
In every doubt, a truth we hold,
Rediscovering grace, a promise bold.

The whispers of the past emerge,
In every heartbeat, we submerge.
Unfurling wings, like doves in flight,
We lift our hearts to endless night.

In every prayer, our souls align,
Finding solace in the divine.
Through trials faced, our spirits soar,
Psalms of love, forevermore.

With gratitude, we write our song,
Rediscovery where we belong.
In faith renewed, our spirits rise,
Together, we embrace the skies.

The Transcendent Dance of Hearts

Two hearts entwined in sacred dance,
Spinning in love, a holy trance.
With every beat, the world dissolves,
In transcendent grace, our spirit solves.

In the rhythm of faith, we sway,
Guided by light, we find our way.
Every movement, a prayer expressed,
In the dance of hearts, we are blessed.

Through every storm, united we stand,
A tapestry woven by heaven's hand.
In each embrace, the universe sings,
The transcendent dance that love brings.

Melodies echo, bright and clear,
Drawing us close, dispelling fear.
In sacred time, together we glide,
In the dance of hearts, love's joy abides.

As stars align in the velvet sky,
We soar through dreams, together we fly.
With every turn, our souls align,
In the dance of life, forever divine.

Divine Emission of Compassion

In the quiet morn, compassion flows,
Sprinkling kindness wherever it goes.
A gentle touch, a soft embrace,
In every heart, we find His grace.

When shadows loom and darkness binds,
Divine emission, love reminds.
Through acts of care, we bridge the divide,
In compassion's light, we take our stride.

With open hands and hearts aglow,
We share the burdens, lighten the woe.
Each whispered prayer, a healing song,
In the web of life, where we belong.

In every moment, let kindness lead,
Planting love's garden, sowing the seed.
From soul to soul, the echoes spread,
Compassion's call, in silence said.

Together we rise, a chorus of grace,
In the divine emission, we find our place.
With every heartbeat, let us impart,
The sacred flame that lives in the heart.

Redemption's Soft Caress

In shadows deep, a whisper calls,
A light descends, where darkness falls.
With tender grace, the heart's embraced,
By love divine, we find our place.

From ashes rise, a spirit pure,
Through trials faced, we will endure.
In every tear, a hope is sown,
To know we are never alone.

The path ahead may seem unclear,
Yet in our souls, God's voice we hear.
With faith as guide, we take each step,
In sacred trust, our hearts adept.

Forgiveness flows, a gentle stream,
Restores the soul, ignites a dream.
In every prayer, our spirits soar,
Redeemed by love forevermore.

So let us walk, hand in hand,
In unity, together we stand.
With hearts aflame, our spirits rise,
In love's embrace, we touch the skies.

Heavenly Echoes of Longing

In quiet nights, we seek the skies,
Where stars collide, and hopes arise.
With hearts attuned to whispers thin,
We yearn for peace that dwells within.

A song of grace, it fills the air,
In every breath, a silent prayer.
We long for truth that never fades,
In love's embrace, our fears cascade.

The heavens part, a promise clear,
In every tear, God draws us near.
With faith as light, we pierce the night,
In sacred dreams, we find our flight.

Each echo sings of joy untold,
A tapestry of love unfolds.
Through every trial, we rise anew,
In heavenly songs, our spirits flew.

So let us dance in sacred space,
Embrace the love, each day we grace.
For in this longing, we shall find,
The light of heaven, intertwined.

Sanctified Bonds of Kindred Spirits

In every heart, a sacred bond,
Where spirits meet, our souls respond.
With kindness shared, we intertwine,
In love's embrace, our paths align.

Through trials faced, our hands entwined,
In shared belief, our hearts aligned.
With laughter bright, we light the way,
In unity, we find our stay.

For every tear we wipe away,
A testament to love's array.
In joys and sorrows, side by side,
In kindred hearts, our faith abides.

With shared strength, we rise anew,
In fervent prayers, our spirits grew.
Together we stand, come what may,
In love's embrace, we will not sway.

So let our bonds be sanctified,
As one we walk, and none divide.
In every moment, here, we thrive,
In kindred spirit, we are alive.

The Rebirth of Starlit Promises

In twilight's glow, a promise reigns,
Rebirth occurs where hope remains.
With every star, a wish takes flight,
In love's embrace, we find our light.

Through darkest hours, the dawn will break,
In every moment, hearts awake.
With faith as guide, we chase our dreams,
In starlit paths, we hear love's themes.

The universe sings a soft refrain,
In silence speaks, through joy and pain.
With every breath, a chance to soar,
In promise held, we ask for more.

Each moment whispers of the dream,
In unity, we share the stream.
As starlit skies begin to glow,
In love's embrace, we come to know.

So let the past anew be born,
Through every challenge, we are sworn.
In starlit dreams that find their way,
We rise in love, forever stay.

Revelations of the Heart's True Yearning

In silence deep, the heart does pray,
Longing for light to guide the way.
Each beat a whisper, soft and clear,
A sacred song that draws us near.

In shadows cast, the truth is bright,
A flicker of love, our soul's delight.
From depths of ache, to peaks of grace,
We find our home in Love's embrace.

With open arms, the heavens call,
To rise from earth, to never fall.
In unity, our spirits soar,
We dance in faith forevermore.

Awakened dreams, sweet visions shared,
In every heart, the flame has flared.
Though trials come, we stand as one,
In every tear, the promise spun.

The heart reveals what eyes can't see,
In longing's depth, the soul is free.
Each revelation, a guiding star,
In love, we journey, near and far.

Chorus of Joy in the Ethereal

In fields of light, our voices rise,
A chorus sweet that fills the skies.
With every note, our spirits play,
In harmony, we find our way.

The laughter echoes, pure and bright,
In sacred moments, hearts take flight.
Beneath the stars, in night's embrace,
We sing our thanks, we seek His grace.

Each sifting breeze, a gentle sigh,
As hope is borne on wings up high.
In unison, our dreams align,
Together here, our souls entwine.

The joy that springs from love's decree,
In every heart, a melody.
We share this bliss, unyielding, true,
In faith's embrace, we start anew.

O'er mountain peaks, through valleys low,
In every step, your blessings flow.
The sacred rhythm of life's song,
In joyous tears, we all belong.

Light After the Darkness: The Sacred Journey

Through shadows deep, we wander forth,
In search of light, the sacred worth.
Each step we take, a prayer in time,
A testament to love's pure climb.

The dawn awakens with tender grace,
Illuminating each weary face.
From trials faced, we rise anew,
A journey blessed, with faith so true.

With whispered guidance from above,
We find our path, we find our love.
In every storm, the calm will wait,
For joy shall come to meet our fate.

The lantern burns, a guiding flame,
In sacred whispers, we speak His name.
Through valleys low, to mountains high,
We walk with courage, hearts awry.

In every heartbeat lies the grace,
To turn our dreams to love's embrace.
Through darkest nights, we learn to see,
The light within, eternally.

Whispers from Beyond: A Reunion of Hearts

From distant realms, the echoes call,
A reunion sweet that binds us all.
In every sigh, a memory stays,
A gentle touch, a love that plays.

The heart remembers what time can't fade,
In sacred bonds, our fears allayed.
With open arms, we greet the day,
In love's pure presence, we dance and sway.

Each whispered promise, a light divine,
In glowing hearts, our spirits shine.
Across the waves, we feel the tie,
The warmth of love that will not die.

Through tearful eyes, we share our grace,
In laughter shared, we find our place.
For every soul that finds its flight,
Will reunite in love's pure light.

With every heartbeat, another starts,
A tapestry woven from many hearts.
Together bound in faith's embrace,
We are one forever in this grace.

Reverent Threads of Celestial Connections

In the stillness of twilight's grace,
We weave our prayers through time and space.
Threads of light bind hearts with care,
Connecting souls in sacred prayer.

Stars above whisper truth so bright,
Guiding us gently through the night.
With every breath, we hold Him near,
In reverence, we conquer fear.

Each moment shared is heaven's song,
In sacred bonds, we all belong.
Eternal love stitched with delight,
In celestial warmth, we find our light.

Faith we gather like morning dew,
A tapestry both old and new.
Bound by grace, we rise and soar,
In His presence, forevermore.

Together we walk on sacred ground,
In unity, His love is found.
Through trials faced, we shall ascend,
In reverent threads, our hearts transcend.

The Sacred Flame of Everlasting Affection

From the heart, a whisper starts,
A sacred flame ignites our hearts.
In every prayer, a soft embrace,
Carried forth in boundless grace.

Flickering bright in darkest night,
A beacon of love, our guiding light.
Through tempests fierce, we hold it high,
In faith, we soar and never sigh.

Each moment shared, a gift divine,
With open arms, in love, we shine.
The sacred fire we can't contain,
In joyful hearts, forever reign.

Together we dance in holy flame,
Each soul ignited, never the same.
Bound by affection that knows no end,
Our lives entwined, forever bend.

In every touch, the warmth of prayer,
A sacred bond, beyond compare.
With unwavering faith, we celebrate,
The sacred flame that won't abate.

Finding Sanctuary in the Arms of the Divine

In quiet moments of deep despair,
We seek His arms, a refuge rare.
A sanctuary of love and peace,
In His grace, all troubles cease.

Like gentle waves upon the shore,
He holds us close, forevermore.
In sorrow's depths, His love appears,
A balm to ease our hidden fears.

With every heartbeat, He draws us near,
In whispered prayers, our hearts revere.
Through trials faced, He lights the way,
In refuge found, we choose to stay.

Together we rise, hand in hand,
In His embrace, we firmly stand.
With faith renewed, we forge ahead,
In sacred love, we are fed.

In every tear, a promise flows,
In sanctuary, compassion grows.
Forever cradled by the Divine,
In His arms, our souls align.

Transcendent Bonds and Sacred Moments

In sacred moments, we stand still,
Feeling the touch of His holy will.
With hearts in unison, we elevate,
Transcendent bonds that celebrate.

Time etched in love, we draw so near,
In every whispered prayer, we hear.
Connective threads, woven with grace,
In unity, we find our place.

Each laughter shared, each tear that falls,
In sacred moments, our spirit calls.
Together we rise, on wings of light,
Through darkness breached, into the night.

In faith we trust, our souls entwined,
In every heartbeat, a love defined.
The world around us fades away,
As we embrace the light of day.

Transcendence flows like rivers wide,
In sacred moments, we abide.
With every breath, we honor, pray,
In love's embrace, we find the way.

Delicate Petals in the Winds of Time

In the garden where the lilies bloom,
Whispers of faith dispel the gloom.
Every petal, a prayer on the breeze,
Carried forth by the gentle trees.

Time flows softly, like a sacred stream,
Each moment a thread in the divine dream.
With grace divine, the seasons turn,
In every heart, a flame does burn.

In twilight's kiss, the stars ignite,
Guiding souls through the velvet night.
In softest tones, the angels sing,
Of love eternal, of sacred spring.

From delicate blooms, our spirits rise,
Reaching upwards towards the skies.
In unity found, joy overflows,
In the breeze where love bestows.

Each petal falls with purpose true,
A testament to all we pursue.
In the winds of time, we find our way,
As blossoms commune in the light of day.

Chronicles of Celestial Passion

Beneath the arch of heaven's grace,
Two souls entwine, a sacred space.
In whispers low, their promises bind,
In the tapestry of fate, they find.

Stars entwined in a cosmic dance,
Echoing the pulse of their romance.
Gathered dreams like beads of light,
In every heartbeat, love ignites.

The age-old tale of kindred souls,
Written in the fabric of their goals.
Through trials faced, the spirit soars,
In passionate verses, forever endures.

With faith as a compass, they set sail,
Through stormy waters, they shall not fail.
Hand in hand, their hearts aligned,
In the chronicles, true love defined.

Time etches stories in the stars above,
Of conquerors, and the power of love.
In celestial realms where dreams ignite,
Together they walk, grace shining bright.

The Holy Grail of Heartfelt Union

In sacred chambers where silence dwells,
Hearts unite, weaving ancient spells.
A chalice raised in the glow of trust,
In love's embrace, they find what's just.

Seeking depths where the spirits blend,
Paths entwined, no need to pretend.
A journey blessed by divine decree,
In each heartbeat, souls roam free.

Through trials faced and shadows cast,
The light of union, forever lasts.
In faithful whispers, they share their dreams,
Of worlds unseen, where hope redeems.

The sacred bond, a radiant flame,
In every challenge, love's the name.
Beyond the veils of time and space,
In the holy grail, they find their place.

From heart to heart, a river flows,
In heartfelt union, true love grows.
In every moment, they rise, they soar,
Together forever, forevermore.

Heavenly Harmonies Reborn

In the symphony of celestial grace,
Melodies linger in this sacred place.
Voices merge in a radiant choir,
Resounding truths that never tire.

Each note a whisper from realms above,
Composed of faith, hope, and love.
In harmony, the spirits sway,
Guiding each heart along the way.

Through valleys deep and mountains high,
The song of the faithful, reaching the sky.
In every heartbeat lies a refrain,
In beauty found, they heal the pain.

With every dawn, a new verse is sung,
Celebrating life, forever young.
Together they dance upon the earth,
In the rhythms of love, they find rebirth.

Heavenly harmonies, forever bright,
Illuminate the shadows of night.
In the concert of life, they find their role,
In sweet unison, they make one whole.

A Sacred Heartbeat in Silence

In shadows deep where whispers dwell,
The silent prayers begin to swell.
With faith as light, we rise and seek,
A sacred song, the heart will speak.

In stillness found, the Spirit flows,
In tranquil night, the wisdom grows.
A gentle hand upon our brow,
Awakens grace, the time is now.

Through trials faced, and burdens borne,
The holy truth, in light is worn.
In every tear, a lesson gleams,
In every heart, compassionate dreams.

The silent hope that fills the air,
An echo of the soul's deep prayer.
In unity, we strive and rise,
Towards the heavens, our spirits fly.

Through sacred heartbeat, we align,
With love that flows, serene, divine.
In quietude, we find our souls,
In silence, Lord, your mercy rolls.

Mythos of the Seraphic Touch

Amidst the flame where spirits soar,
A mythos sings of evermore.
The seraph's touch, in soft embrace,
Transforms the heart with holy grace.

With wings of light, the skies unfurl,
Inviting all to dance and twirl.
In sacred realms where angels tread,
The whispers guide, our spirits fed.

Through trials faced, our spirits grow,
In gentle nudges, love does show.
The mythic tale of faith persists,
Within our souls, the light still exists.

With every sunrise, fresh and bright,
We share the warmth of morning light.
In every breath, a prayer takes flight,
Together bound, in love's delight.

The seraphic touch, a guiding star,
Reminds us we are never far.
In union sweet, our paths align,
In sacred dance, our spirits shine.

Graceful Restitution of Longing

In quiet corners of the mind,
Reside the dreams we seek to find.
With open hearts, we yearn for grace,
A gentle touch, a warm embrace.

Restitution comes, as shadows fade,
In love's pure light, our hearts are laid.
With every heartbeat, longing finds
The strength to rise, our spirits blind.

Through trials faced, we learn to trust,
In faith's embrace, we break the rust.
Restoring hope, our souls ignite,
In unity, we share the light.

Each tear we've shed, a seed that's sown,
In fertile soil, our love has grown.
With every step, the path unfolds,
In graceful arcs, His love upholds.

So let us journey, hand in hand,
In sacred space, together stand.
In restitution, hearts repair,
In love's embrace, we breathe the air.

The Altar of Second Chances

Upon the altar, spirits kneel,
In whispered hopes, our hearts reveal.
The second chance we seek to earn,
In every lesson, our souls discern.

Amidst the rubble, grace will gleam,
In fragile hearts, we find our dream.
With open arms, the past we shed,
In mercy's light, our fears are fed.

Through storms of doubt, we find our way,
In shadows cast, we learn to pray.
The altar stands, a beacon bright,
With every prayer, we chase the light.

In love's embrace, we heal the wound,
With every step, new grace attuned.
In courage found, our spirits rise,
Together bound, to touch the skies.

So here we stand, in faith renewed,
Our hearts ablaze, with love imbued.
The altar waits, for those who yearn,
In second chances, our hearts return.

The Covenant of Infinite Affection

In the silent night, love's whispers flow,
A promise deep as rivers' glow.
Hearts unite in sacred grace,
Bound together, we find our place.

Through trials faced, our spirits soar,
In unity, we tread once more.
The covenant holds, a radiant chain,
Each link a blessing, joy through pain.

In shadows cast by worldly fears,
We walk in light, through laughter and tears.
Infinite affection, ever near,
Guides our steps, dispels the fear.

With hands uplifted, we seek the truth,
In every soul, a spark of youth.
The bond of love, eternally bright,
Illuminates our darkest night.

For love creates, it nurtures too,
In every heart, a life anew.
Together, we share this sacred creed,
In the covenant, we are freed.

Beneath the Wings of Kindness

Beneath the wings where kindness lies,
We find the peace that never dies.
Gentle hearts in tender grace,
Uplifting each in warm embrace.

The weary find a soothing balm,
In loving voices, soft and calm.
A smile shared, a hand to lend,
In each connection, hearts transcend.

With every touch, the spirit grows,
In kindness sown, compassion flows.
Like morning light through trees that sway,
It guides us on our destined way.

Through storms we stand, unwavering, strong,
In unity we sing our song.
For every act of love we spread,
Transforms the world, in kindness bred.

Beneath the wings, together we rise,
With open hearts, we touch the skies.
In every moment, grace defined,
In kindness shared, our souls aligned.

The Resurrection of Fragile Threads

From broken strands, new life will weave,
In fragile threads, we dare believe.
The tapestry of hope and grace,
Emerges from the darkest place.

Each thread a story, softly spun,
In wounds we heal, our battles won.
Resurrected by faith's embrace,
In every heart, a sacred space.

With hands that mend, and hearts that care,
We stitch our sorrows, love laid bare.
In moments lost, redemption found,
Fragile threads in God's love bound.

Together, we rise from ashes low,
In trust we gather, spirits flow.
Resilience forged in trials faced,
Each thread entwined, our lives embraced.

Because from pain, new beauty springs,
In every chord, our spirit sings.
With courage bold, our hearts will lead,
The resurrection of hope's sweet seed.

Faith's Blooming Devotion

In gardens rich with fervent prayer,
Faith blooms brightly, beyond compare.
Each petal soft, a whispered vow,
To nurture love, to live right now.

The morning sun brings life anew,
In every heartbeat, grace shines through.
With every step, devotion grows,
In faith's embrace, the spirit flows.

Through trials fierce, unwavering trust,
In sacred soil, we rise from dust.
The roots of hope hold strong and deep,
In faith's devotion, we shall keep.

As seasons change with sacred song,
In unity, we all belong.
Together, hearts in rhythm beat,
In faith's blooming, we find our seat.

With every prayer, the blossoms spread,
In love's language, all fears shed.
So let us grow, come what may,
In faith's devotion, we find our way.

The Devotion of Time Unraveled

In sacred moments, time stands still,
A gentle touch, a bending will.
We journey forth, both lost and found,
In heartbeats soft, love does abound.

With every sigh, the echoes call,
In shadows cast, we lean and fall.
Through trials faced and joys embraced,
In faithful arms, our dreams are chased.

The ticking clock, divine embrace,
Unraveling threads of hidden grace.
Each passing hour a sacred gift,
With every moment, spirits lift.

As dawn breaks forth, the light reveals,
The truth that time's deep wisdom heals.
In stillness found, our hearts align,
With every breath, the love we sign.

So let us dance upon this thread,
Where love and faith are gently led.
Through all of time, we shall remain,
In bonds unbroken, through joy and pain.

Whispers of the Soul's Embrace

In the stillness where heavens meet,
The heart finds solace, pure and sweet.
With whispers soft as morning dew,
The soul awakens, born anew.

In prayerful silence, dreams take flight,
Guided by the starry night.
Each breath a hymn, a sacred tune,
Beneath the watchful, silver moon.

Voices echo, long and deep,
In faith's embrace, our secrets keep.
As shadows dance, the light bestows,
A touch of grace that ever grows.

In love's embrace, we find our way,
Through trials faced, come what may.
A tapestry of hope, we weave,
In every moment, we believe.

So let us walk this path so true,
In every thrum, the Spirit's hue.
With open hearts as pure as gold,
We share the stories yet untold.

Sacred Whispers of the Heart

In quiet places, whispers bloom,
A sacred space that banishes gloom.
With open hearts, we seek the light,
In love's embrace, the purest sight.

In every tear, a seed is sown,
Through trials faced, we're not alone.
With faith unfurled, we rise and soar,
In whispered prayers, we seek for more.

The heart a vessel, true and kind,
In every moment, love we find.
With gentle hands, we shape our fate,
Each whisper brings us closer, mate.

Beneath the stars, a promise made,
In silence bold, our fears displayed.
The spirit dances, soft and bright,
In whispers sweet, we find our light.

So let the world around us fade,
In sacred bonds, our hearts cascades.
Together as one, we journey far,
In whispers shared, we are the star.

Divine Embrace in the Shadows

In shadowed realms, where silence dwells,
The heart beats soft, and love compels.
In darkest places, light ignites,
A divine embrace that warms the nights.

Through veils of doubt, our spirits climb,
In faith's embrace, we conquer time.
With every step, the path unfolds,
A tale of grace, in whispers told.

Each tear that falls, a prayer released,
In shadows deep, the soul's increased.
With courage found in quiet grace,
We chase the dawn, we seek His face.

The moon above our silent guide,
In every heartbeat, love supplied.
Within our souls, a fire glows,
In divine embrace, our spirit knows.

So let us dwell in shadows bright,
In sacred bonds, we find our light.
Together strong, through thick and thin,
In every shadow, love will win.

Ethereal Paths to Forgiveness

In quiet prayer, our hearts unite,
Seeking grace beneath the light.
Forgiveness blooms in tender soul,
Restoring peace, making us whole.

With gentle whispers, love will flow,
Easing burdens, letting go.
Each tear we shed, a step divine,
Transcending pain, our lives entwine.

As shadows fade, hope's flame ignites,
Guiding us through darkest nights.
The path we walk, a sacred trust,
In faith renewed, our hearts adjust.

Let mercy's touch our spirits blend,
In harmony, our hearts can mend.
With every heartbeat, love's refrain,
Leads us home through joy and pain.

Together we rise, in grace we stand,
A tapestry woven, hand in hand.
In the light of truth, we find our way,
To ethereal paths, come what may.

Celestial Harmony in the Shadows

In twilight's glow, we seek the peace,
Where shadows play and worries cease.
Celestial voices softly sing,
Uniting souls in everything.

Stars align in perfect array,
Guiding wanderers lost in gray.
Each note of love, a sacred sound,
In darkness, light of hope is found.

With hearts attuned to Heaven's song,
We find our place where we belong.
In whispers sweet, the spirits sway,
Bringing dawn to night's decay.

In every heartbeat, grace descends,
Transforming wounds, the soul transcends.
Together weaving dreams divine,
In harmony, our spirits shine.

Eternal dance of light and shade,
A cosmic truth that will not fade.
Celestial harmony unfolds,
In shadows deep, our fate enfolds.

The Sacred Flame Rekindled

In quiet moments, we reflect,
On sacred love, our hearts connect.
The flame within, now gently glows,
A beacon bright where spirit flows.

With whispered prayers, we fan the spark,
Illuminating paths through dark.
In every breath, a promise made,
To nurture what the soul displayed.

As gratitude ignites the fire,
We rise with hope, our hearts aspire.
Restored in faith, we journey near,
Embracing light, dissolving fear.

The sacred flame, a guiding force,
In unity, we find our course.
Transcending trials, love's embrace,
Unites us in the holy space.

In every challenge, grace will bloom,
Transforming all, dispelling gloom.
The sacred flame, forever bright,
Leads us onward, into light.

Spirit's Journey Back to Unity

Through valleys deep, the spirit roams,
In search of peace, in quest for homes.
Each step a prayer, each sigh a song,
In sacred journeys, we belong.

The whispers of the heart will guide,
Uniting paths where love resides.
Every lesson, a thread we weave,
In unity, we learn to believe.

With open hands, we share the grace,
Embracing all in time and space.
In every heartbeat, kindness flows,
Connecting us wherever we go.

Through trials faced and burdens shared,
The spirit's strength can be declared.
In love's embrace, we find our way,
To unity at break of day.

Together we rise, as one, anew,
In harmony, our purpose true.
Spirit's journey, eternally bright,
Guided by love into the light.

Stars Aligned in Sacred Union

Under the vault of the night sky,
Stars shimmer with ancient grace,
Their whispers weave a sacred bond,
Guiding souls to a holy place.

In the silence, a prayer is heard,
Hearts lift like wings to the height,
In cosmic dance, we find our way,
Joined in the celestial light.

Together we seek the divine face,
In the embrace of the starlit glow,
Each heartbeat echoes the truth of love,
In this union, we come and grow.

Through trials faced beneath the stars,
Faith shines bright in darkest plight,
With each step, we conquer fear,
Illuminated by love's pure light.

With every twinkle, a promise made,
A covenant written in the sky,
Together we rise, ever entwined,
As the cosmos sings our lullaby.

The Heart's Pilgrimage towards Unity

On paths of light, we tread each day,
Heartbeats echo in sacred space,
With every step, we seek the joy,
Of finding each soul in its place.

Through valleys low and mountains high,
Our spirits quest for the warm embrace,
In unity's touch, we rise and soar,
Transcending time, we weave the grace.

The journey calls, our feet in tune,
Each moment carved in love's pure fire,
With open hearts, we share our dreams,
In the embrace of the sacred choir.

With every dawn, we start anew,
A tapestry of hope we thread,
Binding our hearts through trials faced,
In this pilgrimage, we are led.

Together we bloom as flowers bright,
In the garden of life's grand design,
With hands entwined, we praise the light,
For in our oneness, we truly shine.

Embracing the Light of Old Flames

In the remnants of fire's warm glow,
We gather the embers of yore,
Old flames rekindled within our hearts,
In the light, we find peace once more.

Whispers linger like softest sighs,
Carrying tales of love's sweet grace,
As memories dance in the twilight,
We embrace what time cannot erase.

Each flicker reminds us of bonds unbroken,
Of promises made in the light of day,
Through shadows cast, our love still glows,
Guiding our journey along the way.

With every heartbeat, our spirits soar,
Reunion of souls destined to meet,
In the warmth of shared laughter,
We find in each other the sacred beat.

In this ritual of life and love,
We honor the paths that brought us here,
Embracing the light of old flames,
In unity, we cast away fear.

The Reawakening of Spiritual Bonds

In silence, the world begins to stir,
Awakening whispers echo through time,
Bound by a thread of sacred trust,
Spiritual bonds in rhythm and rhyme.

Through the veil of the night, we walk,
Hand in hand, the journey unfolds,
With eyes wide open, we perceive,
The beauty of truth that love beholds.

In the tapestry of fate, we thread,
Colors bright woven in prayer,
With each heartbeat, the dawn breaks forth,
Awakening souls, a sacred affair.

As spirits entwine in cosmic grace,
We gather strength from the divine spark,
With every breath, our love ignites,
Illuminating the path through the dark.

In the light of connection, we find our way,
Resurrecting dreams long laid to rest,
With open hearts, we sing in praise,
For in unity, we are truly blessed.

Echoes of Grace in Revered Spaces

In the silence, whispers ring,
Hearts uplifted, angels sing.
Within the stillness, peace descends,
Eternal love that never ends.

Mountains bow and rivers flow,
In sacred trust, our spirits glow.
Gentle breezes speak our prayers,
In reverent hearts, the Spirit shares.

Every tear a lesson learned,
In each struggle, love's fire burned.
Faithful echoes in the night,
Guiding souls toward the light.

Hope resounds in every heart,
From the whole, we shall not part.
In the gathering of the meek,
Divine embrace is what we seek.

Together we shall rise once more,
On the waves, we will explore.
In these spaces, grace renews,
Bringing forth the holy muse.

The Resurrection of Breathless Dreamers

In the shadows, whispers flow,
Dreamers rise from depths below.
Each breath a hymn, soft and clear,
In faith's embrace, we feel no fear.

Turning ashes into light,
In the dark, we find our sight.
The promise of a dawn reborn,
In every soul, the spirit worn.

Lift your eyes to heavens wide,
Where love and grace forever bide.
From the stillness, courage grows,
In the heart, the Spirit shows.

Beyond the veil, we find our peace,
In union, all sorrows cease.
Breathless dreamers claim their place,
In the journey of shared grace.

With each heartbeat, love will soar,
A sacred echo at our core.
In resurrection's morning light,
Breathless dreams shall take their flight.

Together bound, we rise anew,
In every heart, the truth shines through.
With faith the path begins to gleam,
In every soul, a whispered dream.

Sacred Yearning for Reunion

In the garden, prayers arise,
Reaching stars in endless skies.
With every hope, a seed we sow,
A sacred yearning starts to grow.

Echoed hearts, entwined in grace,
Seeking warmth in each embrace.
Through storms of doubt, we stand tall,
In love's embrace, we shall not fall.

The wandering souls find their way,
In dawn's light, we greet the day.
Across the lands, our spirits roam,
In the light, we are at home.

Moments cherished, time to mend,
In every step, we transcend.
Sacred bonds will draw us near,
In every joy, we hold so dear.

As dawn breaks with golden hues,
In reunion, we find our muse.
With hearts ablaze, we seek the light,
In sacred yearning's purest sight.

Illuminated Paths of Everlasting Harmony

Beneath the stars, we find our way,
In illuminated paths, we pray.
With every step, the spirit guides,
In harmony, our faith abides.

Through valleys low and mountains high,
We journey forth, our hearts comply.
In unity, we rise and sing,
To honor love, our offering.

With every breath, the light we share,
In darkness deep, we show we care.
Together, hand in hand, we stand,
In sacred trust, our fates are planned.

The language of the heart we speak,
In every moment, strong or weak.
With grace, the ties that bind us tight,
Illuminate the darkest night.

With visions clear, our spirits soar,
On paths of peace forevermore.
In everlasting harmony,
We find our place, forever free.

Sacred Hearts Singing in the Celestial Realm

In the hush of night, where whispers blend,
Hearts unite in songs that never end.
In the light above, they find their grace,
Voices rise up, in a holy space.

Angels join in, their wings spread wide,
With every beat, the heavens guide.
Unified in love, they chant and soar,
Echoes of faith forevermore.

Stars twinkle bright, in divine chorus,
Each note a prayer, uniting for us.
The sacred dance of spirits entwined,
In celestial realms, their hearts aligned.

From the depths of sorrow, they find delight,
In the arms of the blessed, through the night.
Harmony weaves through the cosmic plan,
Sacred hearts sing, as led by the hand.

Together they rise, in joyous embrace,
In the sacred light, they find their place.
With every heartbeat, love's message swells,
In the celestial realm, where the spirit dwells.

Pilgrimage to the Embrace of Home

Through valleys low, and mountains high,
We journey forth, our spirits fly.
With faithful hearts, we seek the way,
In pilgrimage, we find our stay.

With every step, our burdens release,
In the warmth of love, we find our peace.
Guided by stars that brightly gleam,
We walk together towards the dream.

Each footfall beats with hopes alive,
In the whispers of prayer, we strive.
As shadows fade, and dawn breaks clear,
We draw nearer, our hearts sincere.

The path may wind, yet faith will lead,
To the embrace of home, our souls heed.
In the arms of grace, we shall reside,
With love as our compass, as guide.

Together we stand, in joyful grace,
In the warmth of our love, we find our place.
Through trials and joys, our spirits roam,
In the sacred journey, we find home.

Covenant of Souls: A Journey Within

In stillness deep, the souls convene,
A sacred bond, in realms unseen.
In the quiet whispers, they draw near,
A covenant born, in love sincere.

With each heartbeat, a promise made,
In the depths of trust, they shall not fade.
Journey within, to the sacred core,
In this union of hearts, forevermore.

Side by side, they share their pain,
In the shadowed valleys, love will remain.
Together they rise, as spirits guide,
In the light of grace, they shall abide.

Through challenges faced, they find their way,
In the warmth of truth, they choose to stay.
A tapestry woven with threads of light,
In the covenant of souls, they unite.

With eyes closed tight, they seek the Flame,
In the heart's stillness, they call His name.
In this journey deep, their spirits blend,
In the sacred bond, love knows no end.

Ascension of the Affectionate Spirit

In the dawn's embrace, the spirit ascends,
To the heights of grace, where love transcends.
With wings of light, it soars above,
In the sanctuary of boundless love.

Through trials faced, the spirit grows,
In the dance of faith, the heart bestows.
With every step, it sheds the weight,
In the arms of light, it finds its fate.

In whispers soft, the truth unfolds,
In the language of light, the heart beholds.
With tender grace, it learns to trust,
In the rosy dawn, it finds its must.

The journey steep, yet joy abides,
In every heartbeat, love resides.
With open arms, it greets the morn,
In the ascension, a new spirit born.

In the cosmic dance, we intertwine,
In the glow of love, our hearts align.
To the heavens high, the light shall guide,
In the ascension, forever abide.

A Pilgrim's Path to Reunion

Upon the winding path I tread,
Faith's gentle light before me spreads.
With every step, my heart shall yearn,
For love and peace, my soul's return.

In whispers soft, the heavens call,
Through trials faced, I shall not fall.
For in the distance, hope resides,
A sacred bond that never hides.

With each small act of love I share,
I feel the warmth of blessings rare.
In unity, our spirits rise,
As ancient songs adorn the skies.

The journey long, yet not in vain,
For every joy, I've known the pain.
Yet through the storms, I find my way,
To realms where light shall hold its sway.

As pilgrims join in sacred dance,
In grace, we find our true romance.
For in each heart, a spark divine,
Awaits the day we all align.

Gifts of Grace for the Wanderers

With open hands, the gifts we bear,
For wandering souls, a heartfelt care.
In every seed of kindness sown,
A little light is brightly shown.

Through trials faced and burdens shared,
In silent prayers, we've always bared.
For every tear, a drop of grace,
In love's embrace, we find our place.

Each step we take, a world anew,
In faith and trust, we see it through.
With every heart we meet along,
An echo of the sacred song.

Embracing strangers, hands entwined,
In shared stories, peace we find.
The wanderers, once lost alone,
Now journey forth, forever known.

In gratitude, our spirits rise,
For every gift beneath the skies.
In unity, the path we trace,
A tapestry of love and grace.

The Divine Symphony of Kindred Souls

Beneath the stars, our hearts align,
In harmony, the souls entwine.
A symphony of light and love,
Composed by grace from realms above.

We dance in circles, hand in hand,
In sacred rhythms, we shall stand.
With melodies that softly soar,
Together we unite as one.

Each note a story, each chord a prayer,
In every heartbeat, presence rare.
As kindness echoes through the night,
We find our way by gentle light.

In laughter's joy and sorrow's song,
We weave our paths; we all belong.
For like the stars, though far apart,
We shine together, heart to heart.

Embracing all, in love's embrace,
Transforming pain to healing grace.
With kindred souls, we shall persist,
In this divine, eternal tryst.

An Eternity Wrapped in Tenderness

In tender moments, time stands still,
As love's embrace brings forth the thrill.
With every sigh, a promise made,
An eternity shall not fade.

Through gentle whispers, hearts ignite,
A sacred bond that feels so right.
In dreams we share, our souls take flight,
With hands held tight through every night.

In every touch, a sacred grace,
Each fleeting glance, a warm embrace.
As stars align in cosmic dance,
In love's sweet presence, we find chance.

Through trials faced and mountains high,
With courage true, we learn to fly.
For in the shadows, love will shine,
An endless thread, forever mine.

So let our hearts, like rivers flow,
Through valleys deep, to peaks we go.
An eternity of tenderness,
In heavenly peace, our souls caress.

The Garden of Graceful Encounters

In the stillness of the morn,
We walk the paths of quiet prayer,
With every step, our hearts adorned,
In this garden, love lays bare.

Petals whisper secrets sweet,
The fragrance lifts our souls on high,
In sacred grove, our spirits meet,
Beneath the vast and open sky.

Laughter dances on the breeze,
Like angels in a sunlit choir,
Here, our burdens find their ease,
In the presence of divine fire.

As shadows fade to morning light,
We gather strength from nature's grace,
In unity, we shine so bright,
Within this holy, sacred space.

Each moment blooms, a gift bestowed,
With every breath, a chance to grow,
In this garden, love is sowed,
Where faith and hope forever flow.

Anointed Paths to Rebirth

Upon the road, we tread anew,
With humble hearts, we seek the way,
Anointed souls with visions true,
Embracing light in dawn's soft sway.

Each step we take a sacred trust,
As shadows fade, we rise, restored,
In faith, we turn our doubts to dust,
And follow spirit's whispered word.

Amidst the trials, grace unfolds,
Like blossoms kissed by morning dew,
In every story, love beholds,
The strength that builds when hearts are true.

We shed our skins of yesteryear,
And dance upon the paths we claim,
With joyful cries, we banish fear,
In unity, we sing His name.

As twilight brings the stars to light,
We walk with prayer, our guide above,
Each breath ignites the holy night,
In every moment, we find love.

The Sacred Promise of New Dawn

With every sunrise, hope reborn,
We stand awake, our spirits bright,
In the embrace of day, we mourn,
Yet rise again to seek the light.

In whispers soft, our prayers ascend,
As shadows drift and doubts dissolve,
In sacred trust, our hearts commend,
To find the peace that love resolves.

Each moment spent in grace we share,
A promise written in the sky,
In every glance, a loving stare,
Together, we let sorrow fly.

As colors blend in dawn's first blush,
We gather strength from roots so deep,
With every heartbeat, every hush,
In faith, our sacred calling keep.

So let us rise, hand in hand,
In gratitude, we claim our song,
The world awaits, a vibrant land,
With hope and love, we all belong.

Intertwined in Celestial Light

Beneath the shining stars so bright,
We gather in a circle wide,
With souls embraced in endless flight,
In love's embrace, we gently bide.

For every heartbeat sings His praise,
A melody that knows no end,
In this divine and sacred blaze,
Our spirits soar, our hearts transcend.

With every tear, a river flows,
To cleanse the wounds of yesterday,
In grace, the ancient wisdom grows,
As dawn draws near to light our way.

Each path we take, a holy quest,
In companionship, we find our song,
Together, blessed, we are truly blessed,
In this celestial dance, we belong.

So let our voices rise in praise,
For love unites, our spirits lend,
In harmony, we share our days,
Intertwined, all hearts will mend.

Celestial Indulgence of Togetherness

In cosmic dance, our spirits blend,
A union strong, where hearts transcend.
Celestial dreams, we weave as one,
Beneath the stars, our love begun.

In sacred space, our souls align,
With gentle whispers, love divine.
Together we rise, in joy we flow,
A tapestry of light aglow.

Through trials faced, our bond withstands,
With faith in heart, we join our hands.
In every glance, a promise kept,
In shared embrace, our sorrows wept.

The universe sings, our song of praise,
In harmony bright, we find our ways.
Together we'll soar, on wings of grace,
In every moment, we find our place.

With love as guide, our spirits free,
In celestial realms, just you and me.
In every heartbeat, together we grow,
In endless love, our spirits glow.

Embraced by the Divine Touch

In gentle warmth, He draws us near,
With tender hands, He calms all fear.
Embraced by love, our hearts take flight,
In His divine touch, we find our light.

Each moment spent in stillness true,
Reveals the grace that flows anew.
With eyes wide open, we perceive,
The beauty held in love's reprieve.

Through storms that shake, through trials fierce,
His loving gaze, our doubts disperse.
In every wound, He weaves His thread,
With healing balm, the broken fed.

So let us rise, in faith we stand,
With hearts uplifted, hand in hand.
Together, we bask in love's embrace,
In every touch, His boundless grace.

In whispered prayers, our souls align,
Under the stars, His love we find.
Embraced by light, forever true,
In every breath, we live anew.

Rebirth of the Soul's Flame

In the silence, whispers bloom,
A spark ignites within the gloom.
From ashes arise, the spirit soars,
To dance in light, through open doors.

The heart awakens, love's embrace,
In every trial, find your grace.
With every tear, a seed is sown,
The flame inside has brightly grown.

Infinite sky, vast and deep,
Promises made, for us to keep.
In faith we rise, renewed, and bold,
A story of love, eternally told.

The path ahead, though oft unknown,
In unity, no one alone.
Together we shatter the night,
As souls reunited in purest light.

Let the spirit's warmth guide the way,
Through darkest hours, through light of day.
A circle formed by radiant hearts,
Rebirth begins, as love imparts.

Celestial Bonds Reclaimed

In the tapestry of stars so bright,
We find our kin in the sacred light.
Threads of fate that gently bind,
Hearts united, souls aligned.

Across the heavens, echoes sing,
Of ancient ties that time shall bring.
What once was lost, now found anew,
The cosmic dance, a vibrant view.

Each moment cherished, woven tight,
In every heart, a guiding sight.
The whispers of the winds declare,
That love transcends, is always there.

With every step on this divine plane,
We walk together, joy and pain.
Celestial paths where spirits roam,
In the embrace of love, we home.

Reclaimed is hope, of bonds so dear,
In every laugh, in every tear.
Together, we rise, through each other's grace,
In celestial realms, we find our place.

The Holy Reunion of Kindred Spirits

In sacred space, where souls converge,
A gathering of hearts, a gentle surge.
In silence shared, a knowing glance,
The sacred bond, a timeless dance.

With every heartbeat, echoes align,
In this holy moment, spirits shine.
Here, memories sweetly intertwine,
A reunion blessed, pure and divine.

The warmth of love, a guiding light,
Through shadowed paths, we find our sight.
Each whispered prayer, a solemn vow,
In friendship's arms, we humbly bow.

Together we rise, on wings of grace,
A tapestry woven in love's embrace.
Kindred spirits, through trials, we stand,
In unity's strength, forever hand in hand.

Though paths may wander, hearts stay true,
In every storm, I'll find you.
The holy reunion, a cherished start,
In the language of love, we share one heart.

Resurrection of the Affectionate Heart

From depths of sorrow, where shadows tread,
A tender heart rises from the dead.
In warmth of love, a gentle spark,
Illuminating the once dark.

With every touch, the healing begins,
As fragile hope unfolds from within.
The echoes of laughter, sweet melody,
Restoring the spirit, wild and free.

In each embrace, a promise made,
Reviving dreams that will not fade.
Resurrected joy begins to bloom,
Filling the air, banishing gloom.

The heart's confession, loud and true,
In love's bright light, we start anew.
No more the chains that once confined,
For affection's light, we are aligned.

In unity's grace, we find our way,
With open hearts, we shall not stray.
Resurrection's song, a guiding chart,
In the sacred dance of the affectionate heart.

The Embrace of Eternal Belonging

In shadows deep, a light shall rise,
Guiding souls to heaven's prize.
With open arms, the heart does weave,
A tapestry where all believe.

In silence sweet, His whispers call,
To lift us up, to never fall.
Through trials faced, we stand as one,
In love's embrace, our battles won.

The paths we walk may twist and bend,
Yet in His grace, we find our friend.
Each moment shared, a sacred thread,
Binding us where angels tread.

With hands extended, we gather near,
In every sigh, His presence clear.
Through wounds we heal, through prayers ascend,
In faith, our hearts begin to mend.

Together bound by sacred ties,
We find our home where mercy lies.
Eternal love, our guiding song,
In unity, we all belong.

Carved in the Stone of Faith

Upon the stone, His name inscribed,
In every heart, His love imbibed.
With steadfast hands, we carve our way,
Through trials faced, through light of day.

In every breeze, His whispers flow,
Guiding us where grace will grow.
The burdens lift as prayer ascends,
In sacred trust, this journey blends.

Through storms that rage and shadows creep,
In faith we rise, His promise keep.
The stone endures, as we proclaim,
Our hope renewed in His great name.

By faith we build, through love we stand,
Imprinted deep by His own hand.
The trials faced, the joys embraced,
In every moment, He is grace.

Together, forged in truth so bright,
In bonds of love, we find our light.
In every stone, a story shared,
Our faith remains, forever bared.

Bonds Forged by Divine Will

In quiet prayer, our spirits bind,
Through grace and love, we seek and find.
As rivers flow, our hearts unite,
In sacred trust, we find the light.

Through every tear, a lesson learned,
In faith, we rise, our passion burned.
With every trial, stronger we grow,
In every smile, His mercy flows.

Each hand we hold, a promise made,
In unity, our fears allayed.
Through valleys low and mountains high,
In His embrace, we soar and fly.

With joy, we sing, our voices blend,
In harmony, our hearts amend.
Divine will guides, through night and day,
In bonds of love, we find our way.

Together forged, our spirits soar,
In every heartbeat, we explore.
With faith as fire, we journey long,
In Divine light, we all belong.

The Bloom of Redemption's Heart

From ashes rise, a flower blooms,
In grace, the soul no longer looms.
With whispered prayers, we find our peace,
In love's embrace, our fears release.

Each petal soft, a tale unfolds,
Of mercy shown, of hope retold.
In every thorn, a lesson found,
In trials faced, our hearts unbound.

The sun will shine, the rain will fall,
Through every season, we stand tall.
In faith, we trust, through night and day,
Redemption blooms, our guiding way.

With open hearts, we gather near,
In every sigh, His presence clear.
The bloom of love, forever bright,
In unity, we seek the light.

Let every soul, His glory see,
In every heart, He sets us free.
Together we rise, with hope we'll start,
A garden grown, Redemption's heart.

Sacred Waters of Connection

In the stillness, waters flow,
Carrying whispers of the soul.
Reflections dance, truth does grow,
In sacred pools, we find our whole.

Embrace the grace, the gentle tide,
Where hearts unite, in love's embrace.
With every wave, we shall abide,
In sacred waters, time and space.

Together we rise, spirits soar,
In streams of faith, life intertwines.
Boundless love forevermore,
In sacred waters, our light shines.

Flowing deep as an endless sea,
Each drop a prayer, each wave a song.
In unity, we seek to be,
In sacred waters, we belong.

Let currents guide us, pure and true,
Through every trial, loss, and gain.
A bond eternal, me and you,
In sacred waters, love remains.

Enlightenment in a Symphony of Affection

Hear the echoes of truth resound,
In harmony, our hearts entwine.
Affection's symphony profound,
A melody of love divine.

Voices rise in joyful prayer,
Each note a promise, pure and bright.
Together, banishing despair,
In enlightenment's guiding light.

With every chord, the heavens sing,
In unity, our spirits dance.
The peace that gentle love can bring,
Awakens hope, ignites romance.

Cascading sounds, a flowing stream,
In faith, we weave our sacred tale.
A vibrant tapestry of dream,
In love's embrace, we shall prevail.

Let our hearts be the instruments,
Of kindness, grace, and joy's refrain.
In uplifting moments, recompense,
Together, we'll embrace love's gain.

Traces of the Divine in Heartstrings

Within each pulse, a sacred thread,
Connection deeper than we know.
In heartstrings tied, the light is spread,
A tapestry where rivers flow.

In silent whispers, grace appears,
As love ignites the stars above.
Through laughter, sorrow, joy, and tears,
We find the traces of true love.

With tender hands, we weave and mend,
Each bond revealing life's own grace.
In every moment, hearts transcend,
The divine whispering in place.

And when the darkness clouds our way,
A flicker shines inside our souls.
The joy in unity will stay,
As traces of the divine unfolds.

In every beat, our spirits link,
With love connecting soul to soul.
In heartstrings' dance, we pause and think,
The traces of the divine console.

Journey Through the Labyrinth of Souls

In the labyrinth where spirits roam,
Paths entwined in love's embrace.
A journey leads us far from home,
In every step, we seek our place.

With open hearts and voices clear,
We navigate these sacred halls.
Embracing joy, releasing fear,
Together, heed the ancient calls.

Through twists and turns, the light will guide,
In shadows deep, our faith arise.
Connected by love's gentle tide,
In unity, hope never dies.

In every corner of this maze,
A lesson waits to be revealed.
In the dance of life's tender grace,
Our hearts unfold, our wounds healed.

As souls emerge, through ebb and flow,
We cherish bonds that cannot break.
The journey shared, the love we grow,
In the labyrinth, our hearts awake.

Epiphany in the Garden of Remembrance

In the silence of blooms, whispers fall,
Leaves dance lightly, heeding the call.
Sunlight graces the sacred ground,
In this peace, lost souls are found.

With every petal, a story unfolds,
Of love eternal, and dreams retold.
Here, time halts, in gentle embrace,
In the garden's heart, we find our grace.

Candlelight flickers, memories ignite,
Guiding the weary through the night.
Voices of ages echo and sing,
In the garden's heart, a holy spring.

Amidst the shadows, hope takes flight,
In the dusk's soft glow, all is right.
Hands once parted now intertwine,
In remembrance, love forever shines.

Every tear shed, a seed of light,
Nurtured in soil, they bloom in sight.
With each breath, a promise renews,
In this sanctuary, the spirit's muse.

The Promise of Tomorrow's Dawn

Upon the horizon, a new light glows,
Whispers of hope in the morning's prose.
With every rise, shadows retreat,
In the arms of grace, we find our feet.

The sun beckons, a radiant guide,
Carrying dreams where we abide.
Each moment crafted, a sacred trust,
In the promise of dawn, we place our must.

Birds take flight, on wings of prayer,
Singing praises, rising in the air.
In the gentle breeze, love's embrace,
Bringing forth joy, a sacred space.

With hearts aligned, we walk as one,
In the dance of life, 'neath the sun.
Through valleys deep and mountains tall,
In tomorrow's dawn, we answer the call.

A journey begun, with faith as our creed,
Each step taken, fulfilling the need.
In the glow of the morn, we find our way,
In the promise of tomorrow, we choose to stay.

Testaments of Enduring Affection

In the tapestry of time, threads intertwine,
Every moment crafted, a design divine.
Through trials faced and joys embraced,
In the heart's ledger, love is traced.

Like rivers flowing, ever strong,
Carving paths where memories belong.
In quiet chambers, whispers remain,
Testaments born in joy and pain.

Hands once clasped, now let go,
Yet in the spirit, love will grow.
Through distance measured, hearts unite,
In the dusk of sorrow, stars are bright.

In laughter shared, and tears shed wide,
In every season where love abides.
The bonds that tie can ne'er be severed,
And in the soul's depth, love's ever treasured.

Each word spoken, a vow renewed,
A testament pure, in solitude.
In every heartbeat, echoes remind,
Of love's enduring, sacred bind.

The Altar of Reconnection

Upon this altar, memories stand,
Sacred offerings made by hand.
In the stillness, hearts unveil,
The stories where love prevails.

With open arms and tender grace,
We gather here, in this holy space.
Through trials faced and bridges burned,
In connection found, we have learned.

Candles flicker, illuminating souls,
In shared light, the spirit consoles.
In the warmth of presence, solace grows,
Where love is fierce, and compassion flows.

With words unspoken, we seek the threads,
Binding our hearts, where silence spreads.
In the embrace of kin and kin,
Reconnection blooms, a sacred sin.

Through every season, we rise and fall,
In this sacred embrace, we discover all.
And on this altar, life's grace we find,
In the tapestry of love, forever intertwined.